Master Class

Written by Susannah Bradley
Illustrated by David Mostyn

HENDERSON
PUBLISHING PLC

Creating cartoons

Cartoons are nearly always funny yet they often convey a serious point, too. They look easy to draw, but to draw a really good cartoon takes practice and skill. A cartoonist doesn't just draw what he sees; he shows what he <u>thinks</u> about what he sees as well. Cartoons comment on what they depict by cutting out irrelevant details. In place of any unwanted detail, the cartoonist may draw symbols for emotion, character and movement.

For example, here is an ordinary drawing of a cat.

And here are some cartoon cats. This one is an angry sort of cat ...

...this one is a fat, well-fed cat ...

...and this one is a sleek and elegant cat.

The cat in the ordinary, more realistic drawing may be all of these things but a cartoon will focus on a particular characteristic. It does this by exaggerating those characteristic parts of the cat – the angry cat's claws and fur which stands on end, the fat cat's size and self-satisfied smile, and the sleek cat's smooth shape and elegant walk.

When you draw a cartoon you are saying something. It can be something simple, like: This is an angry cat! or it can be a full story told in a cartoon strip.

Along the right lines

Most cartoons are drawn with simple lines. In this book you will find out how to choose the right sort of lines to show different moods and emotions.

The perfect pencil

At the start of your cartoon career, all you'll need is a pencil and an eraser. Whilst you are learning, an ordinary HB pencil will do the job perfectly. The lead in an HB is neither very hard nor very soft. However, as you progress you may like to try out different pencils. Look at the range shown on pages 46 and 47 for guidance. Meanwhile ...

Pencil posers

If you use a soft-leaded pencil (one which has the number B, or 2B on the side), the marks you make will be easier to erase than those made with a hard pencil (an H or 2H).

For most of your artwork you will need only an HB pencil - which is also fine for tracing. Avoid using the hard H range for roughs - you'll find it hard to erase guidance lines and you won't be able to completely remove any mistakes.

You use a harder pencil (one of the H pencils) for drawing fine lines in clear detail.
A soft pencil (the B range) should be used when you have soft animal fur to draw or plenty of shading to do, as a stronger line is left by these pencils on the paper.

Pen properties

Felt-tip pens are good for going over the pencil lines to make stronger cartoons, because they make an even line as you use them. Other felt pens are good for colouring in, or you can use water-based paints or crayons.

Which paper?

Almost any paper with a smooth surface will do for drawing on. To use an expensive absorbent paper (designed for watercolour work) is a waste of money if you are using only crayons or pencil. Cartridge paper is the best quality for cartoonists to use. Carry a small cartridge paper sketchbook about with you for jotting ideas in.

CARTOON PEOPLE

Head lines

Drawing a head couldn't be easier! The trick is to get all the features into proportion. Begin with a circle. Without pressing down too hard, use your HB pencil to divide the circle into four. These lines will be your guidelines. You will erase them later.

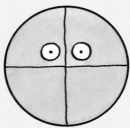

Eyes are positioned each side of the centre, along your horizontal line.

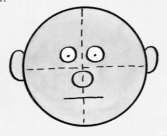

The nose and mouth come in the bottom half, and usually appear centrally on the face. The tops of the ears are level with the eyes.

Add some hair. Think of all the different hair colours, types and styles there are in the world! Try drawing several of them.

Things are looking up....

Now that you can draw a cartoon face which is looking straight at you, have a go at making your person look up or down.

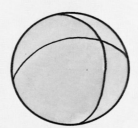

Again, use a ball to draw the guidelines on. Then tilt it in different directions. The lines seem to change. Tilted away from you it looks like this.

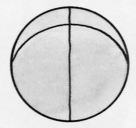

A head, looking up, tilts in the same way.

Tilted towards you, the lines on the ball look like this.

... and down.

Here is a head looking downwards.

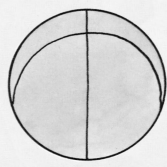

So when you want to draw someone looking up or down, draw your guidelines in the position they would be on the ball.

When a head is turned slightly to one side or another the guidelines will be changed in a different way, like this.

The guidelines help you to place the features correctly, but you can rub them out later. After you've practised for a while, you'll be able to draw a face without using guidelines.

3

A person who is looking up has a nose which curves the other way.

Sometimes the mouth does, too.

And the eyes are much nearer the top of the head than they were when he was looking straight at you.

Someone who is looking down seems to have all his features very near to the bottom of his face. This is because, as he looks down, you can see more of the top of his head and less of his chin.

Neck and neck

Everyone has a neck joining his head to his shoulders.

Some people have long necks – others seem to have no neck at all!

Some people have long, thin heads on long, thin necks and long, thin bodies.

Sometimes their hair makes them look fatter...and sometimes it doesn't.

When you can join a head to a neck and a neck to the top of the body, you can do a Cartoon Portrait! This is the first project for you to try...

Project Page

Draw a self-portrait, cartoon style.

1 Look carefully at yourself in the mirror. Decide whether you have a round look or a long, thin one. Look out for special characteristics, like a pointed chin, a button nose, or a distinctive hairstyle. If the first thing you put on every morning is a baseball cap, you should wear it in the drawing.

2 Start with your head. Draw yourself smiling if you think of yourself as a happy person. But if you want to be seen as a hard case, draw a mean expression. Add spectacles if you normally wear them.

3 Add your neck and the top of your body. What clothes do you like best? Draw them carefully, adding any details of pattern that identify them.

4 Draw a border around the picture. This can be plain or fancy.

5 If you colour your self-portrait be careful to get the skin tones right. This can be difficult with felt-tip pens so be careful. It is better to have an uncoloured portrait than to get it wrong.

Body check

When drawing the whole body remember that people have different ways of sitting, walking and running. When you begin, use single lines for bodies, arms and legs.

The people you draw using these single lines are called stick, or pin, people. And because they are cartoon characters, they can do anything you want them to.

They can do pirouettes on a washing line...

Read a newspaper while hanging by one foot from an upstairs window...

Do the splits and juggle ten balls in the air at the same time.

When you are drawing pin people think about how your joints work. Arms and legs are joined to the body by ball and swivel joints which let you turn them quite freely from the shoulder or hip, but elbow and ankle joints are different – you can only bend them in one direction. Bones in the arms and legs are long and straight, but backbones are made up of many small bones which let you bend, stretch and twist.

Dressing up

Putting clothing onto your pin people is the next stage. The clothes you choose should be appropriate to the character you are drawing... an ordinary old lady is most unlikely to wear leather trousers and a big neon-pink sweater!

Deciding on clothes for your pin person can be a bit like going shopping, because you can choose any clothing you like. Look in magazines or catalogues, or around you at other people to see what people are wearing. Looking at people in the street is best, because there you see people as they really are.

Hands and feet

Pin people wearing clothes need hands and feet! They must look realistic. Hands which are grasping something need to be carefully drawn. Look at your own hand in the mirror, or get someone to model for you, to help you get it right.

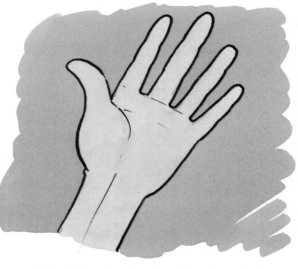

An open hand has the thumb splayed out in the same direction as the fingers,

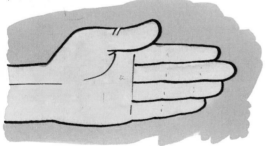

You will see that from one side you can see only the fingers and thumb,

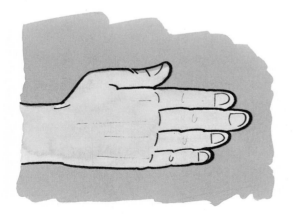

while from the other you can see only the back of the hand with the knuckles showing.

but when the hand grasps something it points in the opposite direction from the fingers.

Setting the scene

People behave differently depending where they are. At an ice rink some people have to throw their arms out to keep their balance. Others glide gracefully along. Some show off, and others cling to their friends... and still fall down! Draw them as pin people before putting clothes on them.

Birds and animals of the same species often move just like each other, but humans rarely do. Travellers studying departure boards are an exception. If you have to wait for a train at a rail station, try to draw your fellow passengers as they study the departure board. They are all very different but what makes them funny is the way they all stand with their heads back, looking slightly puzzled.

Try adding other things to your drawings of cartoon people. Your main character could be a gymnast... or a worker in a burger bar... or a shop assistant and customer at the checkout of a supermarket. The details you choose to draw from these settings help to tell anyone looking at the cartoon more about your characters. As you do this you are making the step towards drawing full cartoon pictures.

See how people sit when they are bored. They fling their arms over the back of their chairs and stick out their legs. How does this differ from the way people sit when they are nervous?

Don't put anything unimportant into your cartoon. It is best kept simple.

Project Page

Draw a pin person frieze to go around your room, or to decorate a birthday card for a friend.

1 Draw two faint guidelines to help you make all your people the same size. You can erase them later.

2 Decide what you want your people to be doing. They could be running a race, or dancing. Some could be holding balloons or flags which you can colour to make the picture more interesting. Make each one different from those next to it.

3 Although most of the heads would be touching the top guide line, some of the people would be bending down a little way. This breaks up the line of heads without spoiling the picture.

4 Allow extra room if one of the people is raising a leg high or spreading out his arms.

5 Let any upraised arms extend over the top line, but keep the feet just above the bottom one.

6 Add skirts to the girls and give some of the characters balloons or flags.

9

Ovals

Now, on to the next stage! Here, we are going to be using ovals instead of stick shapes when drawing our cartoon characters.

One oval will normally do for the body but, if it is to bend at the waist, you may need two.

Because arms bend at the elbows and legs at the knees, each limb will need two ovals, with hands and feet added on as well.

These plumper bodies are easy to draw once you get the idea of how big the arm and leg ovals should be compared to the rest of the body.

Remember, when you see someone from the side, part of the far arm and leg cannot be seen because of the body and the limbs nearest to you.

Compared to adults, babies and toddlers have heads which are bigger in proportion to the rest of them.

How do you view?

Side views look very different from front views.

Bare feet look like this from the front...

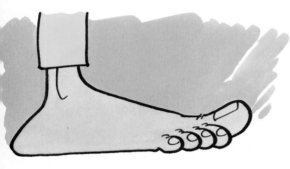

... and like this from the side.

Noses, seen from the side, can look very different from each other.

Teeth can stick out ...

or not be there at all.

Chins become important features from the side, too.

Front on views can be deceptive.

11

Moody characters

Cartoon characters never try to hide their feelings!

By the way you draw his mouth and eyes, you can give a good indication as to what mood your character is in. Someone looking out of the corner of slanted eyes is sure to look shifty, as if they are up to no good. Wide-open eyes never look shifty, but they can look very angry!

Here are some examples of expressions. Copy them and see if you can work out what makes them work. Alter some of the features and see how it changes the expression on that person's face. You'll find that mouths and eyes change the expression quite a lot, but ears and noses make very little difference.

Sad

Happy

Cunning

Nervous

Cross

Furious

Puzzled

Surprised

Project Page

Trace the two cartoon people shown on this page. Use these basic shapes to show expressions like those on the previous page. Make a Rogues' Gallery of faces into a book.

The boxes of eyes and mouths should help you. Choose something from the boxes if you like, or make up your own.

1 Cut out lots of pieces of paper all the same size, and fold them in half.

2 Trace two faces onto each sheet of paper, one each side of the fold, and draw a border around them.

3 Write HAPPY, SAD, or whatever mood you want to show, underneath each picture.

4 Use the best eye and mouth shapes you can find to show each mood.

5 Colour in the pictures.

6 Fold a sheet of card in half for a cover and place underneath the opened sheets. Stitch or staple through all layers along the centre folds. Decorate the cover with the words: ROGUES' GALLERY.

ANIMALS

Animals often appear in cartoons. Just think of all the famous cartoon animals you can see in films!

Elephants

Use ovals for an elephant's body, head and legs. Viewed from the side, only part of the two legs on the far side will be seen.

Add ears and a trunk. The trunk can twist in any direction you like.

Tidy up the edges and add details such as an eye, toenails and a tail.

Seen from the front, a cartoon elephant is drawn in these stages.

Dogs

Dogs are well-known for being bouncy, yappy, and for wagging their tails. These lovable creatures come in plenty of different shapes and sizes. A dachshund is quite different from a Dalmatian, for example.

There are many other such contrasts to choose from. Such differences will give humour to your cartoon.

Artists sometimes give dogs human postures and mannerisms, such as being able to stand up.

Monkeys

Monkeys are similar to humans - their arms, legs, hands and feet are much like those of people - but their faces are different. Therefore you *can* get away with using human limbs for your monkey cartoon, but you will need to learn how to draw a monkey's face.

Here's how to do it:

You should always try to show the character of the creatures you draw. A narrow eye on the look out for a tasty meal makes a crocodile look realistic. Don't forget to draw the big, powerful clawed legs and the ridges on its curved back. Its long nose and sharp teeth are important, too. You need to know a lot about a creature to draw it convincingly, so look at plenty of pictures in books before you start.

Cows, sheep and pigs

Cows are big rectangles with big soppy eyes, and horns.

Sheep are rectangles too – woolly ones. Some sheep have black ears which stick out at the side, and some have black faces.

Pigs look circular from the front, and oval from the side.

Fish

Fish are oval, but have big round eyes, and usually a lot of bubbles drifting away from them, to show that they are underwater.

Snakes

Snakes don't really have eyes which stick up like marbles from the top of their heads, but cartoon snakes often do! The artists who drew Sher Khan, the snake in The Jungle Book film by Disney, gave him a head which turned upwards at an angle from the rest of the body, so that he could turn his head like a human being. He still looked like a snake.

Look at cartoon animals in comics and you will see how stylised the drawing may be while still making the animal look real. Although some cartoon animals wear clothes, they still look like animals.

MONSTERS

Designing cartoon monsters is using your cartoon drawing in the best possible way. Cartoons don't have to look real, so the technique suits the subject. Begin by adapting real creatures and then move on to more imaginative structures.

Man-made Monster

Start with a near-man creation and trace the basic shape onto tracing or greaseproof paper. Work on this until you get the creature you like best of all, then trace it on to best paper.

Use this tracing paper technique from now on for all cartoons. One advantage is that you can use tracings to place a section of a cartoon into a picture wherever you need one. Another is that you can be sure of getting the same likeness another time, without having to worry that you have drawn it the second time too big or too small, or with some of the details wrong.

Your man can change into a monster at the drawing stage by:

turning his hair into spikes

adding craters all over his chest

giving him a tail

altering his feet

changing his expression

Here's another man-monster – trace him and see how many alterations you can make to turn him into a total monster.

Limbs which bend the wrong way or join on to the body in unexpected places can turn a simple creature into a monster. If you want to create a cuddly monster you should make him round, with a happy expression, but a sinister monster needs to be sharp and spiky.

Look at the textures of elephants, toads, and dinosaur recreations to give you ideas for monster skin surfaces.

These can be copied by dipping stubby paintbrushes in nearly-dry paint,

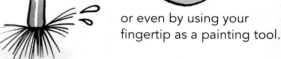

or even by using your fingertip as a painting tool.

If your cartoon monster is large enough you could use a piece of sponge dipped in paint to give you a textured body. Apply it patchily over the area to be coloured and use a second colour in places over it when it has dried.

To merge one colour into another, make fewer dabs with the sponge towards the new colour, then dab the second colour in the gaps and continue with that, getting thicker as you move away from the first colour.

Place a piece of paper over something with a raised surface, such as corrugated cardboard or anaglypta wallpaper, and rub gently over it with a soft crayon. The impression of the pattern will appear on the paper. Use this method of creating skin textures where needed.

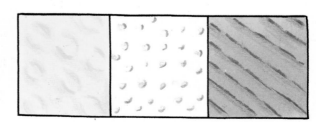

Awful animals

Monsters may be based on animals as well as humans. King Kong is a giant gorilla character from the cinema. His immense size makes him frightening, as well as his expression. To make a monster appear large, you should draw smaller buildings, or people, around him. This puts him in 'proportion'.

Spiders give many people the creeps, so using them to base your monster on is a good idea. Staring beady eyes, hairy bodies and long, angular legs are the parts of a spider which frighten people most, so keep these bits in, but add human features like hands and feet.

Anything thin and angular looks sinister, while plump, round monsters look far more approachable. Use your imagination, and doodle while you think. Some of the best monsters come from doodling. Look at our Nightmare Swan Express, in which victims are swallowed by the demon swan and hurled about the waves in its strange-shaped body.

Two heads are better than one?
Not with this gruesome twosome...

Monsters do not have to look like anything in particular. Blobs of ink or paint can be monster bodies. Use round, white, sticky price labels for eyes, with a black dot in each one for the pupils. Add arms, legs or tails as you need to.

Add scales, hair, scabby bits and scars which still have their stitches in, if you think that your monster still needs livening up!

Gruesome Greeks and other tails

Making monsters out of animals is not a new thing. People were doing it in ancient Greek times, when they frightened each other with tales of the Minotaur, a creature which had a bull's head on a man's body. Their artists drew this mythical creature on the sides of Greek vases, which exist to this day.

Medusa was another Greek monster, said to turn people who looked at her into stone. Her head was alive with writhing snakes instead of hair. Like the Minotaur, she looks especially nasty because she mixes ordinary human features with those of another kind of creature. If you look at the Horoscope symbols, you'll find many more examples of these made-up creatures.

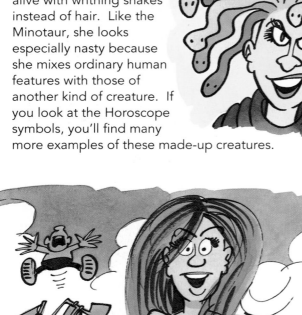

Other imaginary characters from history have survived through the ages to our times. Mermaids do not really exist, sitting on rocks to lure sailors to their deaths, but everyone knows what these half-fish, half-girl creatures look like.

Dragons are very like certain dinosaurs were. It might be that people in olden times, finding dinosaur bones before anyone knew what they were, thought that they were supernatural monsters. This could have added to people's belief that strange monsters really existed. Dragons have a special place in many cultures, and should therefore be treated differently from ordinary monsters.

The Chinese believe that dragons are good creatures. Chinese New Year celebrations always feature huge paper dragons, with men inside them, which dance through the streets. These dragons have cartoon faces.

Most other civilisations consider dragons to be evil, although the Welsh have adopted the dragon as their national emblem. Stories about dragons appear in many children's books and the cartoon styles in which they are drawn vary greatly, showing how artists vary in depicting them.

Project Page

A werewolf is an imaginary creature, often appearing in horror stories or films. It looks like a man most of the time but on nights with a full moon it turns into a wolf.

You can make a flick book to turn into a werewolf and back again. You will need some tracing paper, a pencil, and a magazine picture of a man's head.

1 Lay a piece of tracing paper over the magazine picture of the man. Draw over his features until you have completed the drawing. You should draw eyes, hair, nose, mouth, ears and shape of face.

2 Remove the tracing paper from the magazine picture and place it on a plain white surface. Lay another piece of tracing paper over it and draw over it, but this time change it so that the nose is longer, his mouth becomes a long, thin line, and his face is longer. Raise the position of his ears.

3 Take away the first tracing and place a third piece of tracing paper over the second piece. Change the end of the nose and upper lip to look like that of a dog or wolf. Make the mouth appear open, and add fangs. Narrow the eyes and make the ears even more pointed.

4 Add fur. You can trace this final drawing onto white paper if you like, and colour it with coloured pencils, giving your werewolf sinister red eyes.

5 Trace your Stage 1 drawing onto the first 5 pages of a small notebook.

6 Trace the Stage 2 drawing onto the next 5 pages in the same place ...

... the Stage 3 drawing on the next 5 ...

...and the Stage 4 on the following 5 pages.

Then work backwards through the stages until you have drawn 5 of Stage 1 again.

7 Then, when you flick quickly through the book, the man will change into a werewolf and back again before your very eyes.

19

Animated in animation

Because anything is possible in cartoons, things which are not actually living may be seen to have a life of their own. Cars can have personalities like people – bossy and eager to get everywhere first ...

... or dreamy and slow, trundling along in their own good time.

Again, the cartoonist takes the main characteristic of a car - speed - and translates that into a 'personality' trait.
As well as emotions, car cartoon characters need to be moving.

A fast car may have wheels which slant forward. In real life a car could not keep going with wheels at that angle. But in a cartoon this effect helps the general idea of speed. So do the whizz marks at the back, although in real life these would not exist.

This old van has wheels which look as if they are about to fall off. In a cartoon film, a car like this would probably have bits which came apart on a bumpy bit of road and then fitted together again when the bumpy bit was over.

Metal objects like cars are shiny, even when painted. Show this by shading or colouring your drawing so that you can leave a white line along a surface, as a highlight. This white line is always shaped like the surface it is on, so draw it straight unless the surface of the vehicle is curved, like this:

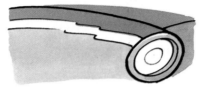

Other inanimate objects may be turned into cartoon characters.

A cup or beaker has a good surface for adding a face. It is round, so draw the shape properly first. To show that it is round, use shading. See pages 47 and 48 for tips on how to do this. When you have drawn a good shape, draw the face on to it, adding shading down one side of the nose. Legs and arms may be added, too. These need to be thin (often the handle is used for an arm, so they should be as thin as that.)

Saucepans and other household items can be brought alive by adding eyes, feet and hands, too.

When drawing saucepans, draw the top and bottom at the same curved angle as each other.

This is wrong...

and this is right.

Robots are machines. One could be based on a vacuum cleaner. Or how about a monster computer with flickering fingers leaping from the disk drive to work its own keyboard?

Door knockers sometimes look like cartoon characters ...

Pictures of old doors can frighten you if there are faces hidden in their wooden depth.

Worst of all is a haunted house, with faces at the windows, bats and spiders all around it, and grasping fingers reaching out of the brickwork ...

Project Page

Make a haunted castle that lights up in the dark!

You will need:

two cereal boxes

greaseproof paper

coloured cellophane sweet wrappers

scissors
felt pens   sticky tape
scraps of white card

bicycle lamp, or torch

1 Cut the long sides out of the cereal boxes. Cut two of them, and make slits in the other two like this:

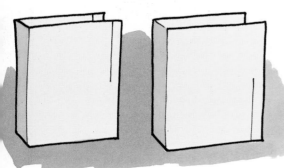

2 Make battlements along the top all round like this.

3 Cut windows in the sides and paint the walls grey. Make wall markings with creepy cartoon eyes in them every so often. Staple real ivy to the walls.

4 Put cartoon figures behind the windows. Draw on to greaseproof paper with felt pens and fix to the inside with sticky tape. Use cellophane for empty windows.

5 Make some cartoon ghosts and put them on the battlements. Make slits in the wall here and there and fix ghosts half in and half out of them.

6 Place your battery-operated light inside and switch on for a spooky effect.

Some tricks of the trade!

Cartoonists may add lines or words which help to convey the mood of the cartoon.

Speed marks show that something is going fast. Sometimes this can be shown as puffs of steam, or clouds of dust. Other times it is just a few straight horizontal lines.

Fright lines wobble. Someone who is frightened may have a worried expression and some fright lines around him to show that he is shaking with fear.

You can even show sound. This opera singer is joyfully booming out an aria, while her dog is barking as if to beg her to stop!

Circular lines show that something is going round, which is a good trick to know about when you are drawing a ballerina, a skater, or a dog chasing its own tail.

Surprise can be shown by tiny dashes around someone's head. This has to be done carefully or they will look like shine marks.

Here is someone seeing stars after a bump on the head...

Accidents look more startling when there are impact marks.

These are shine marks.

And here's someone who can't work out what is going on.

ZIP! BOING! and SPLAT!

Words often appear in cartoons. An accident could have the word CRASH!!! to show extra force.

ZIP! POW! Zoommm! KER-POW!!! All these words indicate great speed. Another trick cartoonists use is to let the character appear to have both feet some distance from the ground. Drops of sweat around his head show that he is putting a lot of effort in.

BOING! is the word to use when something bounces, even if in real life you don't hear a noise like that. Anything which moves fast can have lines to show in what direction it has travelled.

SPLAT! is a useful sort of cartoon word which points out that something messy has happened (it could be one of many things) and gives the idea of what it sounded like.

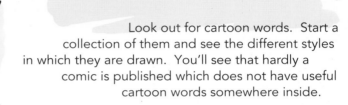

Look out for cartoon words. Start a collection of them and see the different styles in which they are drawn. You'll see that hardly a comic is published which does not have useful cartoon words somewhere inside.

23

LETTERING

Cartoon lettering takes a bit of practice because it must be clear and neat if it is not to let your drawing down.

Decide on the kind of lettering you want to use. Long thin letters which wobble a bit are good for creepy, ghostly effects like Whhoooo- hoo!

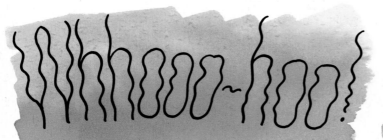

Lettering showing someone going fast needs to be slanted and quite sturdy.

Impact words, like BUMP! and OUCH! can be round and straight, as if there was no chance of getting out of the way. Impact marks around them show the effect even more strongly.

Some lettering is curved. Look for examples of this in comics.

Before you start to put any lettering on to a drawing, practise writing it on tracing paper to make sure it will fit into the space.

LETTERING

Draw guidelines and work out how much space you can allow for each letter. It is worth doing this to avoid having to squash up the last few letters when space is running out. Curve the guide lines if necessary.

ABCDEFG HIJKLMN OPQRSTU VWXYZ

When you have designed a style that you like, make an alphabet of it in an exercise book. You can look through it in the future when you get stuck for ideas.

ABCDEFGHIJ KLMNOPQRS TUVWXYZ

To draw the sort of lettering that appears in speech/thought balloons, you should use a fine black marking pen. Words in balloons are usually written in capital letters which are all the same size. It takes lots of practice to get the lettering even.

Project Page

When you can write in clear, even letters, and draw cartoons too, you'll be able to design some amazing posters!

Here is a poster advertising an after-school football club:

And here's another for the same thing which uses only lettering. The O is a football and the last bit of lettering is written in the grass. Impact lines show that the football is moving and that it has been drawn in the brief moment when it is in the right place in the word.

Most posters are taller than they are wide. When you design a poster, it is best to work at it on rough paper first using a good paper for the final artwork.

Experiment with the following ideas for a Sports Day poster.

1 Write down on scrap paper all the words you will have to put on your poster. Plan to make the name of the event larger than anything else. On scrap paper, write everything roughly, in the sizes you want to use.

You will need to tell people the place where the Sports Day is being held, the date, and the time. If it is to tell people who will take part, you should also tell them who to contact if they need to enter their names in advance for any of the events.

If it is to be put up outside the school, you should include the name of the school. You could put this across the top, in smaller writing.

2 To draw letters like ours, with depth, first draw the fronts of the letters, like this.

3 Then draw the sides, as if they are carved out of stone. The shape you end up with will look rather like a box.

4 Use speed marks when you have drawn the leap-frogger, to show that she is moving fast.

5 Keep any other lettering in neat blocks underneath the SPORTS DAY lettering.

25

Stereotypes

People often look as if they are one 'sort' of person or another. It is dangerous in real life to believe that you can tell what a person is like by the clothes he wears, but it is quite all right in cartoons. These assumptions are called stereotypes. When you look at a stereotype you can tell at once what that person does for a living or what kind of a person he or she is.

Use rounded bodies of the type shown on page 10, and then dress your characters in suitable clothes.

Wedding groups have several different types of people in them. The bride always wears a long white dress and a veil, and carries a bouquet of flowers. A cartoon bride looks either beautiful or quite the reverse. The bridegroom can look glum or happy, and a cartoon one may either be very smartly dressed or wearing clothes which don't fit properly.

Cartoon bridesmaids and pageboys can be sweet or naughty and the bride's mother should carry a big handbag and look a bit sad because in cartoons, mothers always cry at weddings.

Draw the vicar who is marrying the bride and groom. Real life vicars may be young and good-looking, but cartoon ones are old fogies.

A burglar would quickly be arrested if he went around looking like this, but in a cartoon he seems to think he must look the part. His posture, facial expression and clothes give us a number of hints as to what this shifty character is up to.

Does your school teacher wear glasses and a mortar board, and carry a cane and some books with him wherever he goes? Probably not, but it often happens in cartoons.

Ballerinas never walk normally in cartoons – they have to walk on the points of their toes at all times. Her head held high, a ballerina usually has a snooty, button nose.

An artist in a cartoon has to wear a smock, a beret, and have at least three paintbrushes, all dripping with paint, clutched in his hand – as well as a palette.

Think about the things which tell you how a person earns his living. Look at the people shown below and see which item from the box would be needed by each one.

Silhouettes

Some cartoons do not need any details at all – the shading can be total, so that you see people in silhouette.

Silhouette cartoons can be very striking. Because simplicity is all-important in any cartoon, the loss of all detail but the outline helps to make the drawing look strong. But you have to draw a very good outline, as there is nothing else to give the viewer any information.

Here's a cartoon of a street. It is showing the street at night, and all the activity that is still taking place within it. Through the blinds, we can see a silhouette of a large man staggering with an even larger plate of food. Next door, there is a saxophone player sitting behind the curtains, playing a lively tune. The couple next door are drinking wine. We can get quite a lot of information from the silhouettes, without having to see these people in full detail.

Profiles make good silhouettes. You can see from these how a face ages through life, from a baby to an old man. Heads do not grow at the rate of the body, but they get bigger through childhood until they become adult.

Here is a picture of disco dancers. To make this picture, the paper was painted with brightly-coloured inks and, when dry, the outline of the dancers was drawn.

A silhouette in reverse is made by placing a shape onto a piece of paper and spraying colour on and around it. The toothbrush-flicking method of using paint (see pages 46 and 47) can also be used. When the paint has been applied, remove the paper to reveal the white shape. Add eyes and a mouth and you have a cartoon ghost.

Project Page

Design a tablecloth for Halloween which you can use year after year.

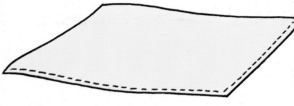

You will need:

a tablecloth made from a plain piece of cotton fabric (hem the edges yourself if you are good at sewing, or ask a grown-up to do it for you on a sewing machine)

tubes of fabric paint

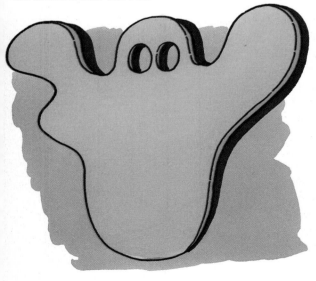

1 Trace the ghost shape on this page onto cardboard and cut out.

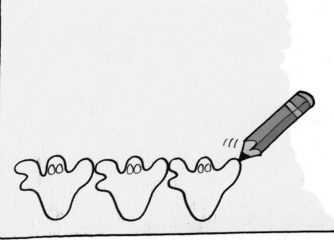

2 Place it just above the hem of the tablecloth and draw around it with the pencil. Move it along a bit and draw around it again. Continue in groups all the way around the edge.

3 Go over the pencil lines with the paints. If you use an unbroken line for one ghost with a dotted line behind it, your ghosts will look more eerie. Add eyes in another colour.

4 Trace the pumpkin shape from this page and use it to make a design in the centre of the tablecloth. Use orange for the pumpkin outline and add the cartoon face details in another colour.

Grid guidance

When you are experimenting with various cartoon characters, you sometimes end up with a drawing which is not as large as you need it to be.

The easiest way of making a drawing bigger or smaller is to take a photocopy of it at a different size, but this is only possible if you have access to a photocopier (your local library should have one).

Another way to make a drawing bigger is to use a grid. Here's how:

1 Mark a sheet of transparent paper into small squares.

2 Fix it over the drawing.

3 Mark a larger sheet of paper into larger squares.

4 Copy what you see in each small square into the corresponding bigger square. The vertical and horizontal guidelines will help to stop the copy getting out of proportion.

If you are prepared for some slight differences when you scale up a drawing in this way, you should have quite a good result.

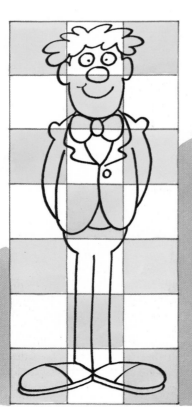

Project Page

Make a moving toy for a child, using a scaled-up drawing of this sailor, or one of your own cartoons.

Scale up the drawing as described on the previous page. Draw the head and body as one piece, but make the arms and legs separate, as shown.

Trace all the pieces onto stiff card. Make holes through circles on arms and legs (not through the black dots).

Cut out and paint all the pieces.

4 Fix the arms behind the body using brass paper fasteners through the black dots on arms and top of body. Fix the legs behind the body using brass paper fasteners through the black dots on legs and bottom of body.

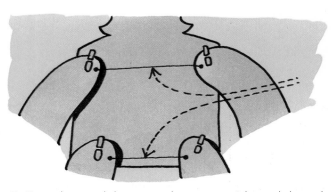

5 Turn the model over to the wrong side and thread string through the arms, tying in a knot as shown. Do the same for the legs.

6 Tie a long piece of string around the string linking the arms, and knot it again on the string linking the legs. Let it hang down.

7 Fix more string through the head of the model and hang up on the wall. When you pull the string, the arms and legs will rise.

Putting things in perspective

Not every cartoon needs a background, but in some cases it can be helpful to have one.

A background can add atmosphere to a cartoon. It can also support the character. It does not have to be detailed – in fact, it is usually better if it is not, because then the attention remains focused on the characters.

Hedges, trees and other countryside scenery is most effective if lightly sketched. Scenery like this should be paler the further away it gets. Distant hills often appear to be a misty blue.

Objects which are the same size as each other appear to get smaller the further away they are. A fence or a row of houses looks like this:

Of course, the fence or row of houses is not really getting smaller. It is an optical illusion, known as 'perspective'. If they went on far enough, they would reach a point on the horizon called the 'vanishing point'. This point is not really there, but it is the place where your vision ends.

So make everything look fainter and smaller, the further away it gets.

Faces in crowds need only be detailed when they are at the front. The rest can be blobs.

Only include what is needed to enhance the cartoon. If the cartoon shows someone in a shop, part of the shop must be shown, so that anyone looking at it knows at once what is happening.

However, even though the background may be sketchy, it should also be accurate. If you have to draw something a little strange to you, look at a picture of something similar to get an idea of how it should look. You should never be afraid to copy a detail from something else into one of your pictures. As long as the picture is your idea, you can use reference from anywhere to improve your work.

Project Page

Design a peephole box using an old shoe box and some extra card.

You will need:

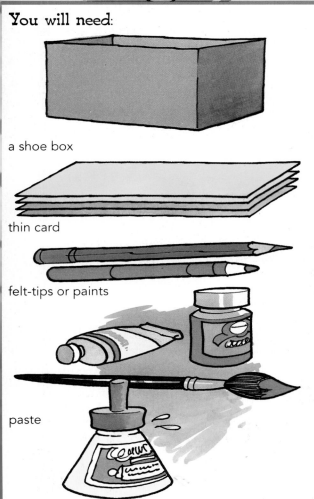

a shoe box

thin card

felt-tips or paints

paste

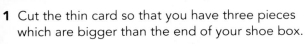

1 Cut the thin card so that you have three pieces which are bigger than the end of your shoe box.

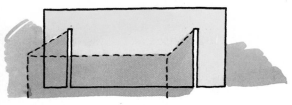

2 Cut slits in them so that they fit over the shoe box, as shown in the diagram.

3 Take them off the shoe box again and cut wavy-edged holes in the centre of each one. The holes should not all be the same shape and size.

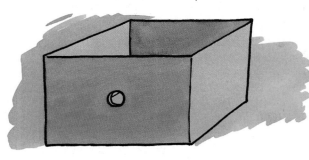

4 Cut a peephole in one end of the shoe box to look through.

5 Now decorate everything with cartoon pictures on any theme you like: it might be a dragon in his lair, or your mum in a deck chair in the park. Draw the dragon, or your mum, on to the inside back of the shoe box. Paste cartoon flowers on to the sheet of card which is to go at the back, and bushes or boulders on the two nearest to your viewpoint, around the holes. You could add some snails and spiders to the one nearest you with your mum in the park – and some elves creeping up on the dragon.

6 Hold the shoe box up to your eye and look at the crazy 3D scene you have created.

33

Cartoon films

Cartoon films are made by lots of artists, all working together to produce one film. Some of the artists work on the backgrounds. Others draw the main characters. Those artists who are good at drawing movement draw the characters in the fast-moving scenes, and others, with a flair for drawing animals, draw any scenes which have animals in them.

They work from a detailed script in which a scene may take up only a few seconds of film time. There are hundreds of scenes in a long animated film. From the script, a set of small sketches is prepared. These drawings are called storyboards, and are used as a guide by all the artists working on the film. By referring to the numbers on the storyboards, which correspond to the scene numbers, each artist can be sure that he is working on the right scene.

Each film uses thousands of drawings. They are all photographed, one after the other, in the right order. The film shows each of these photographs, in turn. They pass across our eyesight so fast that the brain cannot see them separately and so they appear to be one long moving picture.

For one minute of the film, 1,440 pictures are used! These may not differ much from one another but each one has to be separately drawn. This is why so many artists, called animators, work on each film. At all stages, the animators have to check the script to make their characters move to match the sounds which will be present on the soundtrack.

34

Comics

Cartoons are used in sequence in magazines, too. Each cartoon story has a certain number of different pictures, or frames, in which the story is told. First, a writer prepares a story. It must be divided into the number of frames on the page. Usually, each page will have around twelve frames.

Cartoon characters which appear in stories like this have to look the same throughout. Clothes or hairstyles must not be altered unless this happens as part of the story. Characters must not get fatter, or thinner. It is hard to get the same likeness over and over again, so you should practise drawing the same character in different positions.

Stories which are told in pictures do not need many words to describe what is happening, because the picture shows the action. Some picture stories can be told without using any words at all.

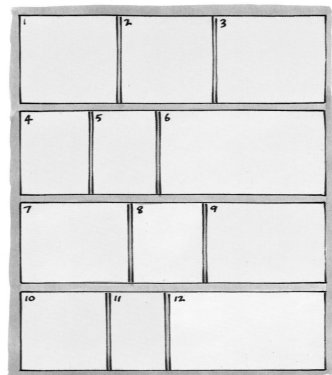

Project Page

Here is a cartoon strip story told in six frames.

1 A boy is happily paddling at the seaside.

2 Suddenly he howls in pain.

3 We can see all of him as he hops out of the sea.

4 The dazed crab sits on the beach while in the background the boy runs up the beach.

5 In a beach hut, he finds a pair of Wellington boots.

6 He happily paddles once again – this time wearing the boots.

Trace the outline of the square provided on this page onto a piece of paper. Trace it five more times so that you have a row of six blank squares.

Trace our illustrations into the squares so that the story can be read in pictures.

Now you have done that, use the page opposite to make up your own story and draw it as a cartoon strip story.

Just joking!

Cartoons are the ideal kind of drawings to illustrate jokes, and some situations appear often. Here are some of the more popular ones:

Desert islands are used in lots of jokes, so there are lots of cartoons of them.

Hospital patients provide us with lots of jokes, like this one:

"Oh, sorry – I thought you were my husband – you look just like him!"

Then there is the walking-along-reading-something joke – here are two versions of it.

Man about to step down an open manhole.
Man approaching a corner with another man also reading something, coming the other way.

Ridiculous realism

Some cartoon film situations could never happen in real life. The Flintstones is a successful show with clever ideas in it, but it ignores the fact that men and dinosaurs never co-existed on Earth. The antics of Popeye the Sailor Man are really funny, but the means by which Popeye outwits Bluto could never happen outside a cartoon scene.

In cartoons, trees land on people and leave them flattened for a few frames (but they still manage to run around). Dogs take bites out of cats, or get their fur burnt off, yet all is back to normal within seconds.

People fall off cliffs and bounce back up again after landing on something sharp, or open parachutes which, until then, you never knew they possessed. Next time you watch a cartoon film, see how much of it is impossible, really.

Plan sequences of events in which crazy things happen to people. Then try drawing them.

Caricatures

Caricatures are very personal cartoons which are meant to look like funny portraits. Daily newspapers often employ cartoonists to draw caricatures of politicians and other famous people. Caricatures exaggerate a person's most prominent feature, so that if someone has a long, pointed nose, the caricature of that person will have a nose even longer and thinner than it is in real life. Bushy eyebrows appear even bushier, and so on.

Artists in big cities like Paris and Florence earn a living by drawing caricatures of tourists at reasonable prices. They set up a stall in the street, and passers-by can watch them at work. The difference between the caricatures they draw and those drawn for the newspapers is that the street artists must never be cruel. Their customers must be pleased with the result – after all, they are paying!

Caricatures are more difficult than ordinary cartoons because there must be a likeness to the real person who has been pictured. Yet they are easier to do than ordinary portraits because you do not have to get all the details right – just the features which you think are most important.

40

Project Page

Do a caricature of one of your friends. You can do it from life if you like (that means looking at them while you draw it). But if you want it to be a surprise, get a photograph of your friend and look at that while you draw. School photographs are excellent for this, because all your worst features seem to show up in them!

1 Before you draw anything, study your friend carefully. What are his or her strongest features? A big chin, or a distinctive hair style? A mouth that looks lop-sided when it is smiling? Everyone has something which a caricaturist can latch on to.

3 Make the most of the features you want to exaggerate. When the drawing is right, go over the lines in pen and colour it in using whatever kind of colouring materials you like best.

2 Sketch the basic shape of the face lightly in pencil. You may decide to draw only the face, but some caricatures show large heads on top of tiny bodies. If your friend has a special way of dressing then this might be the best way to do it.

4 If it is to be a present, put it in a photograph frame – but don't forget to sign it first!

Heart made of ... clay

Cartoons do not always have to be drawn. Sometimes they can be made in Plasticine or clay. Some of the cartoon films you see on television are produced this way. The Plasticine can easily be moved or reshaped so that the character appears to move in film taken of it.

Some advertisers use this technique in their commercials; for example, with a little yellow man rising out of packets of butter or cheese – not really made out of butter, which would not hold its shape, but seeming to be.

Try making a clay or Plasticine cartoon character. If you use different colours, keep them separate, because cartoons are usually bright, not mixed-up. Make sure that the eyes are prominent, because the expression is very important in a cartoon.

Cartooning with collage

Collage is the art of creating pictures by sticking shaped materials onto a background to create an image. There may be no drawing at all in a collage picture. It is a good medium for cartoons because there is little detail needed.

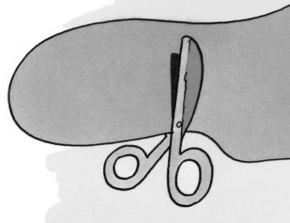

A cartoon ghost may be made of cloth, with felt eyes.

A black felt spider has woolly legs which look really hairy, and big paper eyes.

Different wrapping papers and fabrics give ideas for all kinds of people and animals. If you save scraps of paper and fabric in a cardboard box tucked away in a corner somewhere, you need never be short of materials to create a special collage cartoon picture. You'll save a lot of money on friends' birthday cards, too, if you give them a cartoon collage card you've made yourself.

Collage used with paint gives you an extra freedom to experiment. White paint spattered on to a snowman picture makes it look as if snow is still falling.

43

Papier mâché people

Papier mâché is another technique which is useful in making cartoons. Blown-up balloons, covered in it, make excellent heads to decorate. They can be turned into money boxes, too, by adding a stand made out of an aerosol lid, and cutting a slit to put the money in. The character you make it into could be a person, with the slit in the mouth, or a pig, with a slit in the centre of its back like traditional piggy-bank money boxes. Decorate the 3-dimensional surfaces with cartoon features.

Papier mâché balloons, cut in half, can be fixed to the wall with sticky blue putty in groups, with strings hanging down and tied with a bow near their ends. Before you put them on the wall, draw cartoon faces on them.

You will need:

flour

water

mixing bowl

balloon

1 To make papier mâché, mix some flour and water to a stiff paste in a bowl.

2 Tear old newspaper into small scraps and mix them in.

3 Use this sticky pulp to cover the balloon or to make a shape by itself or on a backing sheet of cardboard.

4 Leave in a warm place to dry out – this could take several hours and you may need to apply several coats. Be sure to wash out the bowl before it sets – it is easier if you don't let it harden.

Project Page

Make a cartoon family tree in papier mâché and collage.

1 Cut out cardboard heads and shoulders for each member of your family, using the patterns on this page. Use the grown-up pattern for every person over fifteen, the child pattern for everyone over one, and the baby pattern for the very tiny people.

2 Cut out and paste on a cardboard nose shape for everyone except the babies. Paste the noses in position with papier mâché pieces.

3 Cover the cardboard with several layers of papier mâché. Leave to dry, then paint the correct skin colour for each one.

4 Cut eyes out of paper and paste in place. (Remember that eyes come about halfway down the head, or you won't have room for the hair.) Add a felt or paper mouth, or draw it on with felt pen.

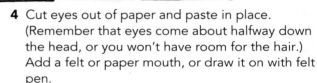

5 Use wool, paper or cotton wool for the hair, and glue in place. Use real fabric for the clothes, adding ribbon, beads or buttons if you like.

6 On a large sheet of card, draw a tree. Cut a trunk and branches out of brown paper or material and stick them over the drawn tree. Add green leaves cut out of fabric, felt or paper. Paste the family members to the tree, with the oldest generation on the trunk, the youngest at the top of the tree, and everyone else in between. Paste a label under each one, with name and date of birth on it.

Keep on practising and you will become a brush-bristlingly brilliant artist, and will soon want to try out different effects. Different kinds of pencils and colouring materials can help you to do this. Here's a selection you should experiment with:

Pencils

Some pencils are hard and make thin, sharp lines on paper. These are marked H to 9H – 9H is very hard indeed.

Soft pencils need sharpening often, because they leave thick lines on paper, and you do not have to press hard to get a strong line. These are marked from B to 9B – 9B is very crumbly!

Ordinary pencils are marked HB. Most of the time you will need only an HB pencil, but for drawing fine lines in sharp detail use a harder pencil (one of the H pencils). The B range should be used when you have soft animal fur to draw or plenty of shading to do, as a stronger line is left by these pencils on the paper.

When tracing, use an HB pencil, as you need a good black line yet one which does not look too fuzzy. Never use one of the H range for roughs, because you will find mistakes almost impossible to erase.

Colouring pencils are easy to handle and can be used for shading - press lightly at first and then gradually heavier. Shading helps to make a character look solid. When using shading you should always decide where the light is coming from. If it is coming from the left of the picture, the shadows and the dark side of the person will always be on the right. Whichever type of pencil you use, you can get good shading effects.

You can also use colouring pencils to blend one colour into another. Go over some of the colour at the place where the two colours meet, lightening the pressure as you go into the other colour. Try to keep your pencil marks going smoothly in the same direction for a neat effect.

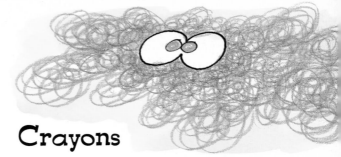

Crayons

Wax crayons are no good for fine detail but come in colours as bright as jewels, which make them good to use in bold cartoons. They are very good for scribble cartoons.

Paint

Paint can be hard to control for beginners. Be sure to use a good paintbrush – the sort which comes to a point. You can buy paintbrushes like these at art shops. They are worth the money because you can paint in more detail with them than with the cheaper brushes.

If you need to get a spattered effect, use fairly dry paint and flick it onto the paper with a paintbrush. Be sure the surface of any surrounding furniture is protected by old newspapers when you do this, and wear old clothes. Wetter paint, used in blobs, makes good Blob Monsters.

Chalk

Chalk shows up well on dark paper. Coloured chalk can be used on both light and dark paper. You can smudge it with your finger to get a blurred effect. Because it rubs away so easily, you should use fixative sprays (see below) to keep the drawing on the paper.

Fine marker pens

Fine marker pens are good drawing instruments – they're delicate and yet leave a strong mark on the paper. Try shading with them by drawing lots of lines going in the same direction. This is called 'hatching'.

Charcoal

Charcoal sticks are sold in boxes, some thick and some thin. There is no outer casing and it breaks easily. It also smudges easily, so you can blur the marks by rubbing them with your finger, and you will have to use fixative on any drawing you want to keep.

Fixative

Fixative for chalk or charcoal drawings comes in aerosol cans or bottles. The aerosol cans should never be thrown on a fire when they are empty. Do not spray them near anyone's face as the fumes are dangerous. Bottles of fixative are used with small metal blowers. You put one end into the bottle and blow through the other. This sort is used in schools so practise there first, if you can.

Felt-tip pens

Felt pens get top marks for ease and cheapness in cartoon drawing. You cannot mix the colours together but that is the only disadvantage. Use thick ones for areas of solid colour and thin ones for drawing lines.

Techniques of the Trade

Cross-hatching

Cross-hatching is hatching done in two directions, one over the other, like this. The shading you do this way is darker than you get with hatching.

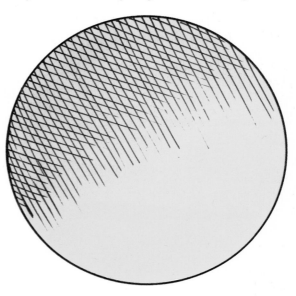

Stippling

Shading using dots is called stippling. There are many other kinds of marks you can make, but they do not have special names. Have fun trying them out!

Your own portfolio

Never throw your drawings away, even if you don't think they are very good. You will learn how to improve your style by looking back on earlier attempts. And they will remind you of techniques you have tried and forgotten about.

Artists keep their work in portfolios, which are big folders made out of rigid plastic sheets or cardboard. You're an artist now, so you'll need one as well! Here's how to make one:

You will need:

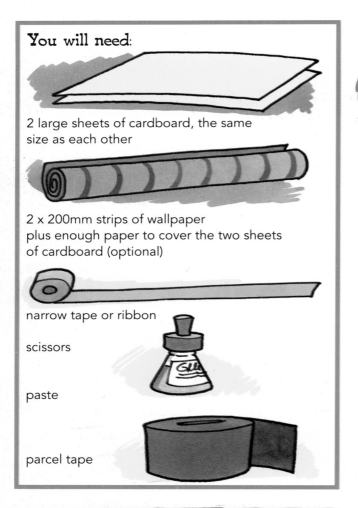

2 large sheets of cardboard, the same size as each other

2 x 200mm strips of wallpaper plus enough paper to cover the two sheets of cardboard (optional)

narrow tape or ribbon

scissors

paste

parcel tape

1 Cover the cardboard with paper (if you've opted to use it) using paste or parcel tape to fix the paper to the cardboard.

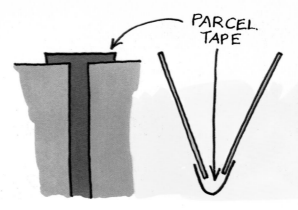

PARCEL TAPE

2 Join them together along one long edge with parcel tape, leaving a gap of 10mm between the two edges to form a flexible hinge.

3 Fold each wallpaper strip into a concertina shape and paste them along the short edges of the portfolio on what is to be the inside.

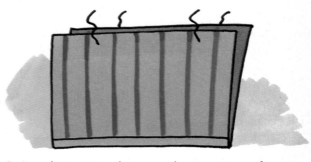

4 Attach tapes to the top edges to use as fasteners.

Your art materials need some protection too, so keep them in a cardboard box or a plastic margarine tub. Protect the bristles of your brushes by making a holder for them out of a cardboard tube, taped up at both ends.

Right then, you've finished.
Ah, but there is one more thing..
start practising your signature - the wackier and more distinctive, the better! Incorporate your style of drawing, like this: